Early Morning - Albert Square

£3.50

Edited by **John Barraclough**

Editorial assistant **Jayne Lanigan**

Written by **Tony Lynch**

design & artwork by **W.H. Print & Design**

additional photography by **Bill Hill**

illustrations by **Jeremy Barlow, John Petts**

Published by **GRANDREAMS LIMITED,** Jadwin House, 205/211 Kentish Town Road, London NW5 2JU.

Printed in Holland.

ISBN 0 86227 384 6

The Publishers would like to thank Julia Smith and the production department of EastEnders for their help in producing this book.

Contents

LONDON BOROUGH OF WALFORD
ALBERT SQUARE

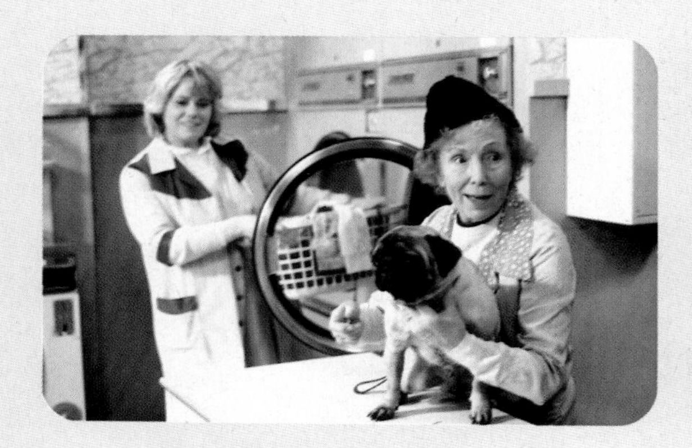

Dear Reader,

Well here it is! Our first EastEnders Special – and I can't wait to look at it myself.

When Grandreams first said they wanted to publish an EastEnders Special I thought "What on earth are they going to put in it?" – but then I started thinking of the past year and a half in Albert Square... of the launderette... the Queen Vic... Den and Angie... Pauline and Arthur... baby Martin – who wasn't even born when we first visited the square, and who is now taking his first steps. And I thought of our friends all over the country and I realized what a great idea it is.

So much has happened since Den put his foot through 'poor old Reg Cox's door'. I wonder what your favourite memories are...? I have so many. Some sad – like the cot death of baby Hassan. Or happy memories – like Pauline's face when she found her son Mark. And, almost best of all, Arthur looking after all three babies: Annie, Martin and Vicki. But this book isn't about the past. It's a sort of "celebration of EastEnders" that will make us both remember 1985 & 86 and look forward to 1987... in Albert Square, in the London Borough of Walford.

I mustn't keep you any longer. Happy Reading!

From myself and all the EastEnders

(Julia Smith)
Producer

Meet the EastEnders

They say that Wales is the land of song, but there's nothing to compare with a good old-fashioned Cockney knees-up and when the residents of Albert Square get together in their local, The Queen Vic, a right old sing-song and a good time is had by all.

IT TAKES ALL SORTS

Just as part of the success of EastEnders is the blending together of a variety of characters, so here the actors and actresses who portray the 'youngsters' in the series prove, that *to make a world...*

	Letitia Dean	Susan Tully	Shreela Ghosh
	Sharon	Michelle	Naima
Birth place	Wild Hill, nr. Hatfield	Highgate, London	Shillong, Assam, India
Home at present	Near Regents Park	Highbury, London	Central London
Nickname and reason for it	Tisha — a short version for Letitia	None	Sona (means 'gold' — precious — first daughter in the family for 3 generations)
Favourite Actor	Paul Nicholas	Denholm Elliot	Harry Dean Stanton
Favourite Actress	Meryl Streep	Beryl Reid	Lauren Bacall
Favourite Singer/Group	Phil Collins, Wall Street Crash, Alison Moyet	Too varied for favourites	Aretha Franklin, Tina Turner
Favourite Sports Personality	Jimmy Greaves	Dennis Taylor	Vivien Richards, John McEnroe, Ilie Nastase
Favourite Food	Italian. Fresh salad	Anything Chinese	Guacamole
Favourite TV Show	Just Good Friends. Dynasty	Hill Street Blues	Newsnight, Spitting Image
Hobbies	Swimming, collecting Doris Day records	Tapestry	Weight training, Indian classical dance, eating out
Superstitions	Not walking under ladders	None	Read Patrick Walker in The Standard every day
Ambitions	To make a successful situation comedy. Make a record	—	To be a great mother and work in movies

Tom Watt	Nick Berry	Paul J. Medford	Adam Woodyatt	Linda Davidson
Lofty	Wicksy	Kelvin	Ian	Mary
Wanstead, East London	Woodford Green, Essex	London	Thorpe Coome Hospital Walthamstow. 28/6/68	Toronto, Canada
Finsbury Park, London	Islington	London	—	Flat in North London
Elwood (From the movie The Blues Bros., Nick Berry being Jake)	Jake (Tom Watt is Elwood). We are The Blues Bros.	Mr. Rivers, Joan Rivers' husband	Itchy — Itchy Ban is Japanese for first born so my Dad called me Itchy Titchy 'cos I was small	Boo: Ever since I was born the guy who lived in the flat above us called it me
Robert De Niro	Clark Gable	Dustin Hoffman Michael Douglas	None	Too many to mention
Juliet Stevenson	Vivien Leigh	Valerie Harper	Michelle Pfeiffer from Scarface	Wendy Richard, Bette Davies
Talking Heads	Billie Holliday	Maze	U2	Liza Minnelli, Bob Geldof, Ben Vereen
Viv Anderson	Trevor Brooking	John McEnroe	Jimmy White	Steve Perryman
Ice cream	Peanut butter sandwiches	Mexican	Deep pan pizzas	Steak and big fat chips
Channel 4 News	Old Movies	Hill Street Blues	Brookside	Lovejoy, Kojak, Little House on The Prairie
Swimming, Watt the Duck Records, reading History	Beating Tom Watt at table tennis and most sports, theatre. Old movies	Horse Riding, Skiing, Tennis	Snooker, motorbikes & survival	Ballet, decorating my flat, going to the theatre
None	None	Every one you can think of	I won't ride my motorbike on Oct. 12th as I have fallen off in '84 and '85 on that date	Loads — never to whistle in my dressing room etc.
To make movies	To make movies	To be extremely rich, but not too famous	To get a 147 break in snooker, I'll never do it though	To be able to sing — well

ANGIE WATTS really deserves better than her husband Den. But deep down and despite everything, she really does love him. Angie is the driving force behind the 'Queen Vic' — the pub just wouldn't operate properly without her. Angie is portrayed by the lovely Anita Dobson, a native of Stepney.

DEN WATTS is a real snappy dresser, and a bit of a Jack-the-Lad, too. He is the landlord of the Queen Victoria pub, and he isn't averse to a spot of fiddling on the side. Much to the distress and annoyance of his long-suffering wife, Angie, Den is also a notorious womaniser. Leslie Grantham, one of Britain's leading heart-throbs,gives a great performance as "Dirty Den".

The Babies

Here are the newest arrivals in Albert Square. . .

Martin

When Mary Smith first realised that she was pregnant, she believed it would spell the end of the world. But these days, and despite everything, she can't imagine a time without her lovely little Annie. . .

Lou Beale went bonkers when she first heard that Pauline was expecting another baby — at her age indeed! But of course when Martin Albert Fowler came along, she was the happiest Grandma in the world.

Later on, when Michelle presented her with baby Vicki, our Lou became the happiest *Great* Grandma in the world, too!

Michelle and Vicki (above)
Mary and Annie (right)

Ali

Turkish Cypriot ALI OSMAN runs Al's Cafe in Bridge Street. Trouble is, he gambles away most of the profits. At least he would, if wife Sue didn't keep an eagle-eye on him at all times. Ali is played by Nejdet Salih who was born in London in 1957.

Sue

Sure, SUE OSMAN is ambitious. But she's not all that ambitious. She just wants to get on in the world. Her main drawback is husband Ali, whose lazy streak and liking for the inside of a betting shop always seems to hold them back. Sue is portrayed by Sandy Ratcliffe.

Wicksy's Cocktails

Wicksy says that cocktails don't have to be alcoholic. Next time you have a party, picnic or barbecue, why not give these non-alcoholic EastEnders specials a try ?

Purple Cloud

Fill glass with ice cold milk

Top up with Kia-Ora Blackcurrant Health Drink

Stir and drink immediately

Sparkling Blue

Put ice in a large tumbler

Add a measure of Kia-Ora Tropic-Ora

Fill glass with Sparkling Malvern Water

Serve with slices of orange and lemon

Sharon's Surprise

Fill glass half full with American Ginger Ale

Add a tablespoon of vanilla ice cream

Top up with Lemonade

Pour into jug and whisk all the ingredients together until frothy

Pour back into glass

Bridge St. Bonanza

Put ice in a large tumbler

Add one third Bitter Lemon

Add one third Original Ginger Ale

Fill glass with Limon

Serve with a slice of lemon

Pete's Fruity Fizz

Put ice in a large tumbler

Fill half full with Appletise

Top up with the juice of a freshly squeezed orange

Serve with slices of apple, cucumber and orange

Den's Delight

Put ice in a large tumbler

Add a bottle of Tonic

Fill with Sparkling Orange and Passionfruit

Serve with a slice of orange

Wicksy's Wonder

Put ice in a large tumbler

Add a bottle of American Ginger Ale

Add a bottle of Tonic

Fill up a glass with Sparkling Orange

Serve with an orange slice

Contrary Mary

Put ice in a tumbler

Fill two thirds full with Tomato Juice Cocktail

Top up with Tonic Water

Add a shake of Worcestershire sauce

Stir

Party Cola

Put ice in a large tumbler

Add a measure of Kia-Ora Blackcurrant Health Drink

Fill with Pepsi Cola

Serve with maraschino cherries on a stick

Lean Lofty

Half fill a glass with ice

Pour over Slimline Tonic

Add a dash of Angostura Bitters

Stir well and garnish with a slice of lemon

Iced Ginger Tonic

Pour American Ginger Ale into an ice cube tray and freeze

Fill glass with Tonic

Add ginger ale ice cubes

Serve with a slice of lemon

Summer Refresher

Put ice in a tumbler

Add a bottle of Grapefruit Juice

Fill with Lemonade

Serve with a slice of lemon

Long Cool Lime

Put ice in a large tumbler

Add a dash of lime

Fill glass with Lemonade

Serve with a slice of lemon

Recipés and illustrations supplied by Schweppes.

Who lives where

The Tower Block

Ian Beale

Mother and Father,
Pete and Kathy

Nº 23

Mary Smith

daughter Annie

Nº 3

Kelvin & Cassie Carpenter

Mother and Father,
Hannah and Tony

The Queen Victoria

Sharon Watts
Mother and Father,
Den and Angie
Simon Wicks

Nº 45

Michelle Fowler
daughter Vicki
Mother and Father,
Pauline and Arthur
brothers
Martin and Mark
(who has now left home);
grandmother,
Lou Beale

Nº 1c

Lofty (George)
Holloway

He's mean, selfish and aggressive. He'd shop his own granny for a fiver (or less). He's NICK COTTON, the EastEnder you just love to hate, and the bane of poor Dot's life. 'Nasty Nick' is played by John Altman.

Dot

DOT COTTON — leads a lonely old existence. Deserted by her old man and put-upon by her son Nick (whenever he decides to come home that is!), she finds life to be quite a trial these days. And all those aches and pains don't help much either, as she'll readily tell you. Dot is brilliantly portrayed by June Brown.

As Michael Caine, another well-known Londoner, might say -

EastEnders Facts File

. . . There are two real Albert Squares in London. One in E15, the other in SW18.

. . . The artwork which forms the background to the title sequence of EastEnders measures 9 feet by 7 feet. It is a compilation of more than 1000 aerial photographs of the real East End.

. . . The 'LONDON E20' postal distr

. . . Each character in EastEnders has a full wardrobe of work and leisure wear. This is supplied and maintained by the Costume Department.

. . . The original EastEnders characters were created by producer Julia Smith and script editor Tony Holland.

. . . It takes a week to shoot two episodes of EastEnders

. . . There are three real Bridge Streets in London — in NW6, SW1 and Richmond.

. . . Oscar Jam

. . . 17 members of the EastEnders cast were actually born in London.

. . . The total number of people — actors, technicians and production staff — working on EastEnders is 95.

. . . Walford is of course a fictitious borough. However, village called Walford exist in Worcestershire and Shropshire.

. . . Peter Dean (Pete Beale) used to work in a funfair.

. . . EastEnders scripts are written at least 30 episodes ahead of transmission.

“Not a lot of people know that. . .”

. . . Bill Treacher (Arthur Fowler) was once a steward on an ocean liner.

. . . Peter Dean and Letitia Dean are no relation whatsoever. Neither are Linda and Ross Davidson.

oes not exist.

. . . Gretchen Franklin (Ethel Skinner) played Alf Garnett's wife in the original pilot show of 'Till Death Us Do Part'.

. . . Sandy Ratcliffe (Sue Osman) played bass guitar in the rock bands 'Tropical Appetite' and 'Escalator'.

. . . Anita Dobson (Angie Watts) once worked as a juvenile model for C&A.

ony Carpenter) is a practising Shoushu Buddhist.

. . . Nejdet Salih (Ali Osman) spoke no English until he was five years-old.

. . . Ross Davidson (Andy O'Brien) used to be a PE teacher.

. Leslie Grantham (Den Watts) a connoisseur of fine wines.

. . . 31 scriptwriters have worked on EastEnders.

. . . Wendy Richard (Pauline Fowler) appeared as the female voice on Mike Sarne's No. 1 hit record 'Come Outside'

. . . Approximately 20 million viewers watch each episode of EastEnders.

Pete

You could trust dependable PETE BEALE with your life. He is Pauline Fowler's twin brother, and he runs the fruit and veg stall in Bridge Street. Pete — the life and soul of any party — is portrayed by Peter Dean.

Kathy

KATHY BEALE — played by Gillian Taylforth — is Pete Beale's second wife. She needed all her reserves of strength and her sense of humour when dealing with the initial reaction to her in Albert Square. Kath helps out on Pete's fruit and veg stall and she works part-time in the 'Queen Vic'.

WHEN THEY

Before they became famous as residents of Albert Square, many members of the cast already had established acting careers.

This is Anita Dobson long before she became Angie of the Queen Victoria.

Anglo-EMI Films

Sandy Ratcliffe, Sue Osman, was once a fashion model and also a film actress, as she appears here in 'Family Life'.

The first 'silly old moo' of 'Till Death Us Do Part' was Gretchen Franklin now Ethel Skinner.

Also shown l/r Una Stubbs, Tony Booth, Warren Mitchell.

WERE YOUNG

These youngsters are now all EastEnders regulars. Can you spot who they are? Answers on page 61.

1(?)

2(?)

3(?)

EastEnders Quiz

1. Who tussled with the drag artist in the Queen Vic?
   a. Den;
   b. Arthur;
   c. Dot Cotton;
   d. Pete Beale.

2. Where was Andy O'Brien born?
   a. Glasgow;
   b. Edinburgh;
   c. Isle of Arran;
   d. Carlisle.

3. Who lives at No. 45, Albert Square?
   a. The Carpenters;
   b. The Fowlers;
   c. The Watts;
   d. Dr. Legg.

4. What is Ethel's surname?
   a. Skinner;
   b. Wilson;
   c. Shaw;
   d. Hills.

5. What were the names of Debbie's kittens?
   a. Starsky and Hutch;
   b. Little and Large;
   c. Pinky and Perky;
   d. Cagney & Lacey.

6. What was the name of the knitting firm set up by Lofty, Ian and Kelvin?
   a. Albert Enterprises;
   b. Youth Unlimited;
   c. EastEnd Fashions;
   d. Loftellian.

7. Who lent the knitting machine to them?
   a. Hannah Carpenter;
   b. Debbie;
   c. Kath;
   d. Pauline.

8. One of the Square's residents is a would be clairvoyant. Who is it?
   a. Ethel;
   b. Lou;
   c. Dot;
   d. Ian.

9. Who pestered Debbie with anonymous 'phone calls?
   a. Ali;
   b. Saeed;
   c. Kelvin;
   d. Tony.

10. Who offered to be the business advisor to Lofty & Co. in their knitting enterprise?
   a. Den;
   b. Pete;
   c. Simon;
   d. Debbie.

11. What is the name of Dot Cotton's husband?
   a. Alfred;
   b. Jimmy;
   c. Willie;
   d. Charlie.

12. Where did Michelle and Lou go for a holiday?
   a. Southend;
   b. Margate;
   c. Ramsgate;
   d. Clacton.

13. What colours are worn by Walford Town? (The Wallies)
   a. red & white;
   b. claret & blue;
   c. black & white;
   d. blue & white.

14. In the Walford Carnival who played 'Black Death'
   a. Sharon;
   b. Mary;
   c. Ethel;
   d. Debbie.

15. What is Lofty's real christian name?
   a. George;
   b. Gary;
   c. David;
   d. Tony.

16. Who questioned Nick about the death of Reg Cox?
   a. D.S. Quick;
   b. D.S. Rich;
   c. D.C. Evans;
   d. W.P.C. Alison Howard.

17. Who stole cash from *The Queen Vic?*
   a. Lofty;
   b. Wicksy;
   c. Kath;
   d. Sharon.

18. What was the name of the male stripper who appeared at *The Queen Vic?*
   a. Fancy Freddie;
   b. Fabulous Frankie;
   c. Fearless Freddie;
   d. Fantastic Frankie.

19. Who did Lofty hit with a boomerang?
   a. Ethel;
   b. Lou;
   c. Den;
   d. Dot.

20. Where does Dr. Legg live?
   a. Albert Square;
   b. Hackney;
   c. Hampstead;
   d. Islington.

21. Who took over the flat of Reg Cox when he died?
   a. Ali and Sue;
   b. Dot;
   c. Mary;
   d. Lofty.

22. What is the name of Pete Beale's first wife? (Simon Wicks' mother)

a. Jennie;
b. Dora;
c. Pat;
d. Shirley.

23. Which EastEnder appeared in a T.V. beer commercial as a guardsman?

a. Arthur;
b. Pete;
c. Den;
d. Lofty.

24. Which EastEnder appeared briefly in the T.V. epic 'Jewel in the Crown'?

a. Peter Dean (Pete);
b. Leslie Grantham (Den);
c. Anna Wing (Lou);
d. Shreela Ghosh (Naima).

25. When Michelle 'invented' a holiday boyfriend what was his nationality?

a. Irish;
b. Spanish;
c. Italian;
d. Swiss.

26. In episode I who punched his fist through the glass in the pub door?

a. Ali;
b. Den;
c. Nick;
d. Tony.

27. What nationality is Ali?

a. Turkish/Cypriot;
b. Cypriot;
c. Greek;
d. Albanian.

28. What was Lofty doing before coming to Albert Square?

a. barman at Southend;
b. car mechanic in the army;
c. hotel porter in the West End;
d. male nurse in a hospital.

29. When Reg Cox was found dying in his room who found him?

a. Den, Lofty, Arthur;
b. Den, Ali, Arthur;
c. Pete, Ali, Arthur;
d. Nick, Ali, Den.

30. What colour is Simon's sports car?

a. red;
b. green;
c. yellow;
d. white.

31. Who gave Lofty a special hair cut & blow dry which was a disaster?

a. Michelle;
b. Mary;
c. Pauline;
d. Sharon.

32. Who accidentally soaked W.P.C. Alison Howard with a hosepipe?

a. Kelvin & Ian;
b. Arthur;
c. Nick;
d. Ali & Sue.

33. What was the name of Mary's stripper friend?

a. Diana;
b. Julie;
c. Sheena;
d. Tracey.

34. How did Nick get access to Dr. Legg's medical records?

a. he broke in;
b. Ethel let him in;
c. he found them in the Square;
d. he copied Ethel's key.

35. What's the name of Dr. Legg's house?

a. Homeleigh;
b. Cromer;
c. Cranleigh;
d. Ventnor.

36. What is the name of Sue and Ali's Cafe?

a. Ali's Cafe;
b. Bridge Cafe;
c. Al's Cafe;
d. Albert Cafe.

37. Where did Den and Angie go on their ill-fated holiday?

a. Ibiza;
b. Benidorm;
c. Majorca;
d. Estartit.

38. How many Albert Square Street signs are there in the Square?

a. 3;
b. 6;
c. 1;
d. 2.

39. How were Ethel's parents tragically killed at the same time?

a. gas leak;
b. doodle bug;
c. train crash;
d. motor accident.

40. Who returned Willy to Ethel after he was lost?

a. Dot;
b. Kelvin;
c. Den;
d. D.S. Quick.

Answers on page 61

Famous Fan

Daredevil **Eddie Kidd** watches no other soap but EastEnders.

Irish songbird **Rose Marie** is a real 'Dirty Den' fan. "He's a real cracker! As my old mate Frank Carson might say."

Heavyweight **Frank Bruno** thinks EastEnders is the 'punchiest' soap of them all . . .

After Penny Lane, Strawberry Fields and the Mu of Kintyre, Albert Square ranks pretty high amongst **Paul McCartney's** favourite places. . .

The realistic cockney accents appeal to **Nick Heyward.**

Sally Thomsett 'escapes' from the world of T.V. and films by regular 'visits' to Albert Square.

Tony Knowles would be well and truly snookered if he missed too many episodes of his favourite soap opera . . .

When Princess Anne presented the 1986 Top TV Personality awards to Anita Dobson and Leslie Grantham, she confessed that she didn't know who they were! The Princess was in the minority, though, for EastEnders is enjoyed by approximately 20 million viewers every episode. Among them are a number of famous fans . . .

Status Quo's **Rick Parfitt** really enjoys EastEnders. He says "EastEnders is the most natural down-to-earth show I've seen on T.V."

Sexy **Samantha Fox** always finds the time to curl up in front of the TV when EastEnders is on . . .

EastEnders Cook Book

Thanks to the cosmopolitan influence of its multi-racial society, London's East End now boasts some of the finest cuisine to be found anywhere in the city. Here, four EastEnders present the truly international flavour of Albert Square by giving you their own recipes for a favourite homeland dish...

Ethel's Eel Pie

Ethel Skinner just loves the traditional cockney dish of eel pie:
You will need:

1 skinned Eel.

Puff pastry (available ready to cook).

Some egg glaze.

1. Slice the eel into pieces approx 1½" long.
2. Season the pieces with salt, pepper and sage.
3. Lay the eel pieces in a pie dish.
4. Cover with puff pastry.
5. Lightly brush the pastry with egg glaze.
6. Bake the pie for 20 minutes at Gas Mark 7-8 (425°- 450°) until the crust rises and is nicely browned.
7. Lower the oven temperature to Gas Mark 5 (375°) and cook for a further half hour.

Ali's Turkish Coffee

It's an old tradition in Ali Osman's family to drink Kahwa, or Turkish Coffee. Traditionally this drink is made in a 'brik', but it can be made just as well in a saucepan:
To make enough for four cups, you will need:

4 teaspoons of sugar.

4 cups of water (filled to the brim).

4 heaped teaspoons of Turkish coffee, ground almost to powder.

1 cardamom pod, cracked.

1. Boil the water and sugar in the saucepan.
2. Add the coffee and cardamom pod.
3. Stir well, returning to the heat.
4. As the coffee froths up to the rim of the saucepan, lower the heat.
5. Repeat the 'frothing' *twice.*
6. Allow the grounds to settle.
7. Remove the cardamom pod.
8. Serve very hot, topping up each cup with some of the froth.

Naima's Iced Tea Cocktail

Naima often likes to relax with an ICED TEA COCKTAIL, cool and refreshing after a long day in the shop:
You will need:

3 ice cubes.
1 tablespoon of rosehip syrup.
1 tablespoon of lemon juice.
1 tablespoon of sugar.
1 tablespoon of pineapple juice.
1 tablespoon of orange juice.
Soda water.
Cold tea.
Slices of orange and lemon.
Bottled cherries.

1. Place the ice cubes into a ½ pint stemmed glass.
2. Pour in the rosehip syrup.
3. Gently add the lemon juice, sugar, pineapple juice and orange juice one-by-one.
   If you are very careful you'll be able to achieve a very attractive 'layering' effect.
4. Top up with soda water and cold tea. *Do Not Stir.*
5. Add a slice of lemon and orange, together with a couple of cherries.

Dr. Legg's Gefilte fish

In Dr. Legg's very strict Jewish household Gefilte fish was always a treat for Friday evening. This very tasty treat may be used as a main course or starter. To make enough for 4

2 lb. fish—a mixture is best: white fish, such as carp, haddock, cod, and whiting; rich fish, such as herring, mackerel, bream (only use about ½ lb. of rich fish).
1 carrot.
3 medium sized onions.
2 teaspoons salt.
pepper.
3 tablespoons (3¾T) matzo meal, or white breadcrumbs.
1 teaspoon sugar.
2 eggs.

1. Ask the fishmonger to fillet and skin the fish, but take bones, head and skin; wash fish, the bones and skin are for making the stock.
2. Prepare and slice carrot and onion. Put the fish bones, head, skin, carrot, 1 onion, 1 teaspoon of the salt and a shake of pepper into a pan and cover with water. Cook for about 20 minutes.
3. Mince (grind) the fish with the other two onions, and the bread, if used. Mix together with the salt, pepper, sugar, and beaten eggs and matzo meal, if used.
4. With wetted hands, make the mixture into 14-16 balls and place them in the fish stock. Simmer gently for 1 hour or longer. Remove the fish balls from the stock, place on a plate and decorate with slices of the cooked carrot. Strain the stock, chill and serve separately.

Delanie Forbes .... ***Cassie Carpenter***

As Cassie Carpenter, 10 year-old Delanie Forbes plays the youngest *speaking* character in EastEnders (unless of course you count the occasional gurgles of the three babies!). This is a challenge that's admirably met by this talented young actress.

Delanie was born in May 1976, at Sidcup in Kent. She wanted to be an actress from the moment that her elder brother, Gary, enrolled at a London stage school. Although her professional career actually began when she appeared on the cover of a video cassette at the ripe old age of 1½! Two years later she made her TV debut in a play for the BBC.

When she isn't appearing in EastEnders, Delanie attends a school in Mottingham, south-east London. She is also a part-time pupil at the Sylvia Young Theatre School where she polishes up her acting and dancing skills.

Delanie would love to continue her acting career when she gets older — and who knows where the constantly developing character of Cassie Carpenter will lead her?

Paul J. Medford .... ***Kelvin Carpenter***

Paul J. Medford was all set to go west — to America — when the part of Kelvin Carpenter was offered to him. "I was going to study drama in Washington — but EastEnders was an offer I just couldn't refuse," he remembers.

Paul was born in west London, of Barbadian parents, in November 1967. He attended stage schools — Barbara Speake and Italia Conti — for ten years. He has appeared in several feature films and had several TV roles under his belt when 'Kelvin' came along.

Nowadays young Kelvin Carpenter is a well-established EastEnder. He's a lad with a good head on his shoulders and he manages to cope with most things that life throws at him — usually from the direction of his parents, Tony and Hannah!

Pauline

No matter what life holds in store for kind-hearted PAULINE FOWLER, she always seems to pull through and emerge with a smile. Pauline is portrayed by that ever-popular actress Wendy Richard.

Arthur

ARTHUR FOWLER — played by Bill Treacher — has had more than his fair share of life's ups and downs. He's known redundancy and he's stood his turn in the dole queue. Son Mark and daughter Michelle have given him plenty to worry about, too. But Arthur's pride and joy are his wife Pauline and baby son Martin.

Nick Berry .... ***Simon Wicks***

Acting-wise, Nick Berry is perhaps the most experienced of all the younger members of the EastEnders cast. He was born in April 1963 at Woodford, Essex, and learned his craft at the Sylvia Young Theatre School.

One of Nick's early stage successes was in the hit musical *Oliver* at London's Albery Theatre — with which he also toured all over Britain. When the show was later revived at the Aldwych Theatre, Nick was in that cast, too. His other theatrical successes include roles in the Greek drama *Orestes* at Woolwich, and in the sophisticated comedy *Why Me?* at the Strand Theatre in the West End.

Nick has also been seen on the big screen, in the movies *Party, Party*; *Forever Young* and *Leave it To You O.K.?*

TV viewers have seen him play lead roles in *Rip it Up* and *Purple People Eater*. He has also appeared in *The Gentle Touch*, with Jill Gascoine, *The Audition*, and in the visually stunning *Box of Delights* in which he played King Rat.

Nowadays, Nick's time is occupied almost entirely by the sometimes cool, sometimes confused character of the Queen Vic's barman 'Wicksy' — a part that he plays with a fine understanding.

Linda Davidson .... *Mary Smith*

Mary Smith is a northerner, from Stockport. She came down south to make a new start for herself after having a baby at 18. The Health authorities found her the room in Albert Square which she shares with her lovely daughter Annie.

Life is tough for Mary. Not only is she an unmarried mum, she also has difficulty with reading and writing. In the past she has hidden her true personality under various punkish disguises — but sometimes, just sometimes, the real Mary shines through.

Mary is portrayed by Linda Davidson who came to the north of England from Canada, where she was born in 1964.

As a child she studied ballet, and in 1980 she travelled south to attend the Italia Conti Stage Academy. She remembers her time there as a particularly happy experience.

Between leaving drama school in 1984 and joining the cast of EastEnders, Linda appeared in several TV dramas.

Linda finds Mary to be: "One of the saddest residents in Albert Square, and that makes her a very interesting character to portray."

The Building o

Albert Square was once no more than a sloping patch of mud and sand on the back-lot of the BBC's studios at Elstree in Hertfordshire.

The site before building commenced.

Mike Hagan (Construction Manager) and Keith Harris (Senior Designer).

Overseeing the building of the square was senior designer Keith Harris, who had spent the past 19 years working on various BBC productions. "Even so," he said, "the unique opportunity to design a full-size Victorian square was a really tremendous challenge."

Indeed, Albert Square was to be one of the largest exterior sets ever built for a British TV production. "It was rather like leaving TV to work on a feature film," said Keith. "Except that our square had to be designed to last through a much longer life span than does the average film set."

From the outset, Keith worked closely with producer Julia Smith and script editor Tony Holland. As the storylines developed, so too did the ideas for the homes and habitats of the characters.

One of the first things to be decided upon was the exact siting of the street and houses in the square. "A great many factors had to be considered," said Keith. "The direction of the sun, for instance, and the neighbouring tower block which now forms part of the permanent backdrop to Albert Square."

Also taken into consideration was the amount of possible 'nuisance' that the set might cause to the surrounding neighbourhood. "After all, no one wants a view of a 35 foot brick wall from their living room!"

And so, taking all these points into account, Keith Harris took the first steps in the birth of Albert Square, by drawing up his first plans — with a stick in the sand!

The next step was the draining of the site via an elaborate system of trenches which would also carry cables for camera pick-up points around the square.

Cardboard models were then produced and discussed, together with plans for the interior sets.

A great deal of research went into the quest for accuracy and realism. This included following exact proportions, as laid down by Victorian architects and builders.

Many photographs were taken of real Victorian squares in Hackney and Bethnal Green. "These served to spark off ideas on general proportions and some aspects of the finer decorative detail," said Keith.

In May the site was cleared ready for the building of Albert Square. Outside contractors were called in to carry out the 'hard landscaping' of the site — laying drains, road and pavements, and erecting the steel framework for each block of dwellings.

The outer shell of each building in the square was made by a small army of craftsmen in the BBC's construction workshop. These shells, made of plywood and plaster, were then bolted onto the rigid framework.

When finished, each structure, or block, was complete on at least three sides. Inside each one, at the first floor level, is a metal platform used for any action involving characters at an upstairs window. Each of the buildings is strong enough to withstand high winds or heavy gales — even the roofs are fully strengthened — in case the storyline calls for a roof-top chase!

A thousand-and-one other details had to be attended to: period doors were brought in from a demolition company, sash window frames were constructed, together with authentic-looking drainpipes, chimney stacks and window panes. Even details of the brickwork are authentic, being made from fibre glass moulds taken from a genuine East End brick wall. The same method was used for fine detail in archways, lintels, bay windows, and of slates and pilasters.

Albert Square

Its remarkable transformation into Britain's most famous set of late-Victorian dwellings began in February 1984.

The Queen Victoria unadorned.

The shell of 'pillar box' row where Mary and Dot Cotton live at No. 23.

Once the set was erected, it then had to be 'aged' — after all, it was supposed to have stood there for more than a hundred years. This was achieved in a number of ways: pavements were deliberately chipped and cracked, paintwork was given a gnarled, uneven look by means of a special chemical which cracks the top coat, damp patches were added to the underside of the railway bridge by using varnish, garden walls were made to sag and so on.

The finishing touches were finally added towards the end of the summer 1984 — a telephone kiosk and telegraph pole from British Telecom, lamposts from the Hertsmere Borough Council, and several cars and vans to park in the streets.

The overall effect is quite remarkable, and the greatest compliments for the design and construction teams often come from visitors to Elstree, when they ask, 'Where is the set?' as they cannot believe that Albert Square isn't real.

While the exterior set was being created, work was also under way on the interiors. The Queen Vic, Al's Cafe, the launderette and Lou Beale's house were among the first to be built.

In each set, all appliances — gas, water, etc. — are fully functional. For instance, Sue and Ali could actually cook you a meal, Pauline could do your laundry, and Angie could pull a pint of genuine beer for you.

The design of each interior began with a thorough study of the characters who would 'live' within its walls. As with the exterior, attention to detail was the keynote to a successful effect.

All the props — furniture, curtains, crockery etc. – were chosen with great care so as not to be at odds with the tastes of the characters using them. In the older homes everything had to have its own history of marks, stains, sags, scratches and so on – so that the viewers accept and believe in them, just as they believe in the characters who make EastEnders so enjoyable.

The end result

Letitia Dean .... *Sharon Watts*

Lovely Letitia Dean, who plays Sharon Watts in EastEnders was born at Campfield Place in Hertfordshire in 1967.

Letitia and her elder brother Stephen were both stage-struck youngsters. They attended dancing school together when the family moved to Buckinghamshire.

At the age of 12 all of Letitia's hard work and training paid off when she won the coveted role of 'Pepper' in the West End hit musical *Annie.*

Since then her acting career hasn't looked back. She has appeared in numerous TV programmes including *Love Story, Tales Out of School, Brookside, Relative Strangers, The Bill* — she also played 'Lucinda' in *Grange Hill.* Letitia still loves singing and dancing too, and has starred as 'Sandy' in the stage musical *Grease.*

But of course the high spot of her career to date is her portrayal of Sharon Watts, adopted daughter of Den and Angie in EastEnders.

"Poor old Sharon, sometimes she doesn't know which way to turn," says Letitia. "She loves both her mum and her dad, but they always seem to be at odds with one another. And being adopted doesn't help much either. Sometimes she feels very insecure — no wonder she goes over the top now and again!"

Tom Watt .... *Lofty Holloway*

Lofty Holloway, barman at the Queen Vic., is a sad, almost pathetic figure. His life has been full of disappointments and setbacks and he is thought of by the other residents of Albert Square as a bit of a wash-out despite his well-meaning ways and his obvious heart of gold.

He used to be in the Army, but was discharged on medical grounds — a condition known as dormant asthma.

Lofty is portrayed by Tom Watt, a native of Wanstead. Tom studied drama at Manchester University where he directed several stage productions. He has appeared many times on the professional stage and has had several juicy roles on TV, including Duane the Punk in the comedy series *Never the Twain.*

"Lofty is a fascinating part to play," says Tom. "To see how this seemingly insecure character develops from episode to episode. I admire his guts, and the way he battles with his innate shyness."

The Pets

King Roly of the Queen Vic ▼

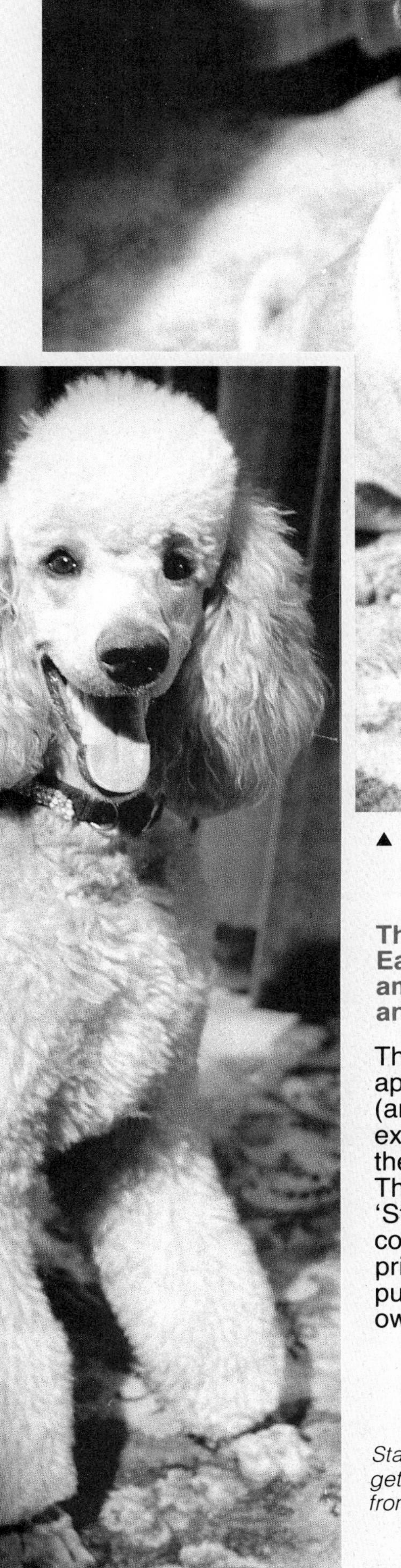

▲ *Willy —*
a pug with a mind of his own

The pets featured in EastEnders must be among the most famous animals in Britain.

There's 'Roly' the Watts' apricot standard poodle (and Den's quickest excuse for getting out of the house!).
There's Debbie's cats 'Starsky & Hutch', and of course there's Ethel's pride and joy 'Willy', a pug with a mind of his own.

Starsky and Hutch as kittens get a well-deserved cuddle from their proud owner Debbie ▶

Adam Woodyatt .... *Ian Beale*

Once upon a time Adam Woodyatt seriously considered a career as a butcher. "That was my Saturday job," he recalls, "and I'd learnt a lot about the trade. The regular customers all knew me and I could tell them what meat was the best value."

But then Adam was offered the part of EastEnder Ian Beale, son of Pete and Kathy. Naturally he grabbed it with both hands.

Adam was born in Essex in 1968 and had studied drama at the Sylvia Young School. He first appeared on the West End stage in the 1980 revival of the great musical *Oliver* in which he was a member of Fagin's gang of young thieves. From there he went on to appear at the National Theatre in *On the Razzle* which starred Felicity Kendal.

On TV he was seen as 'Shiner' in the children's drama series *The Baker Street Boys* and he played 'David Firkettle' in *The Witches and Grinnygog.*

Nowadays Adam greatly enjoys portraying Ian — and we certainly enjoy watching him. Butchery's loss was most definitely an EastEnders gain.

Susan Tully .... ***Michelle Fowler***

What with one thing and another Michelle Fowler has had the most traumatic time of all the EastEnders youngsters.

"She's certainly had to grow up fast," says Susan Tully who plays Michelle on screen. "And now she's got baby Vicki to cope with, too."

Susan, born in north London in October 1967, is well qualified to take on such a challenging role. She had studied drama since the age of 7 and made her first TV appearance two years later on *Our Show*. After that came live appearances on *The Saturday Banana Show* with Bill Oddie. "That was really terrifying," remembers Susan.

Other TV parts followed, and a feature film starring Petula Clark. Then Susan was offered the part of the rebellious 'Suzanne' in *Grange Hill* which she played for four series.

These days Susan is as anxious as the rest of us to see how the character of Michelle develops. "I hope she makes a success of bringing up her child — I think she deserves it, don't you?"

One of the most important units in the EastEnders production team is the make-up department, headed by make-up designer Shaunna Harrison. The department is responsible for the facial 'look' and the hair style of each character.

"Most of the cast have a 'no make-up' look," explains Shaunna, "with the exception of Angie Watts, who obviously takes a great deal of time and care over her glamorous looks."

The hair styles for most of the cast are ordinary everyday hair styles as seen on any East End street. But even these vary, from the 'home-perm' look of Lou Beale to the 'salon-styled' look of Angie Watts and the blonde streaks of Kathy Beale.

Whenever possible the department styles the artistes own hair and very rarely resorts to the use of wigs. "Although Ethel Skinner does have an acrylic pull-on wig — for Sunday-best wear only," says Shaunna.

A detailed file of notes and Polaroid photographs are kept for reference purposes on the make-up of each EastEnder. "In years to come it will be interesting to look back and see how fashions have changed, and the way that characters have aged and developed," says Shaunna.

The four faces of Mary

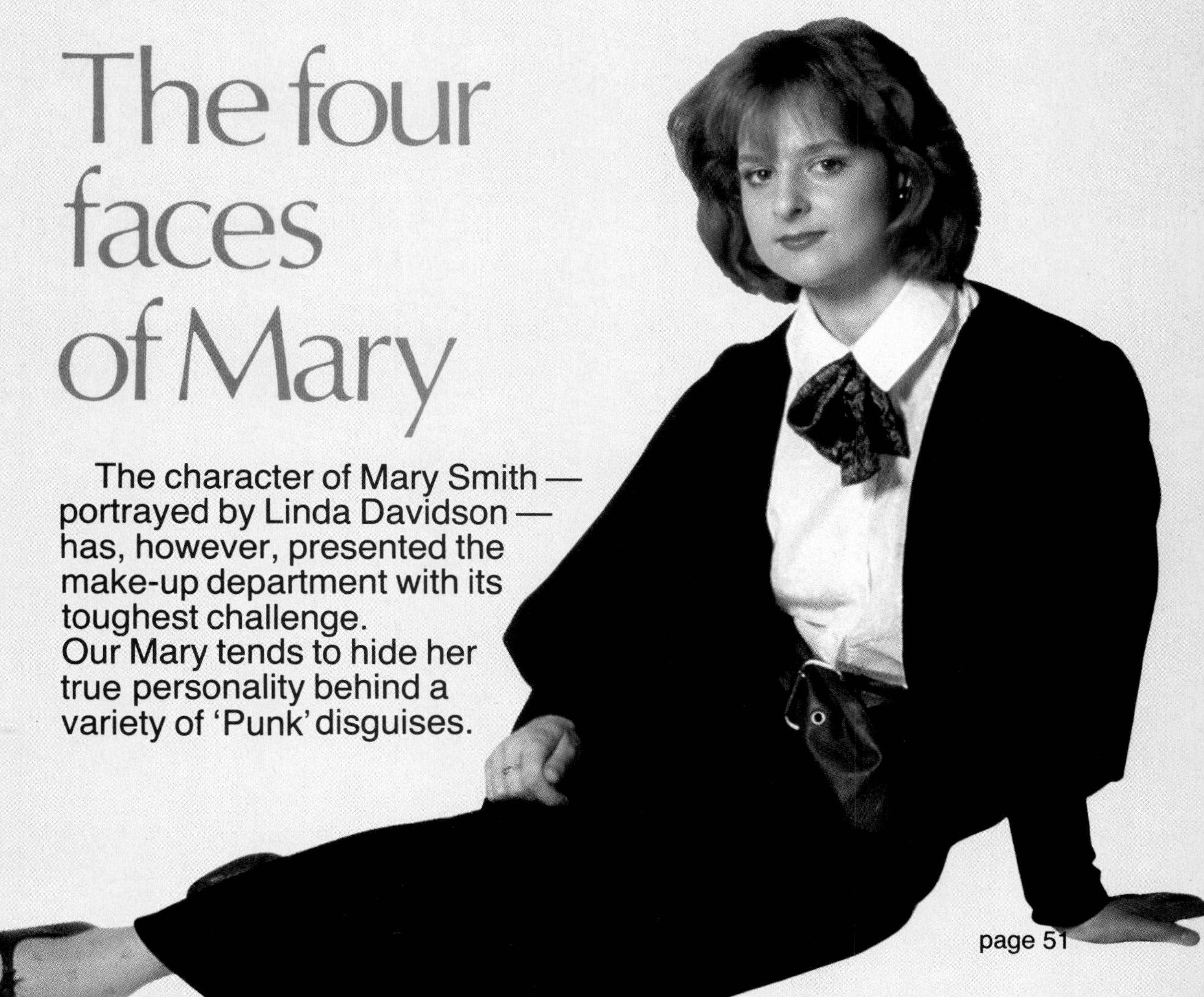

The character of Mary Smith — portrayed by Linda Davidson — has, however, presented the make-up department with its toughest challenge. Our Mary tends to hide her true personality behind a variety of 'Punk' disguises.

Debbie

DEBBIE WILKINS — a girl with big ideas, scrimped and saved to raise a mortgage on No. 43 Albert Square. When she first arrived the other residents thought her a bit stuck-up and toffee-nosed. They never guessed that she came from a Walford council estate less than two miles away. Debbie is portrayed by Shirley Cheriton.

Naima

Since the failure of her arranged marriage to Saeed, NAIMA JEFFERY has become a more independent young woman. Despite all the obstacles, she is determined to make a success of the foodstore in Bridge Street. When she isn't involved in shop business she likes to read the classics. Naima is portrayed by Shreela Ghosh.

The Senior Citizens

Watching EastEnders, you get the feeling that Albert Square has a real history behind it. This is largely due to the masterly creation of the older characters — Lou Beale, Dr. Legg, Dot Cotton and Ethel Skinner.

Between them they have seen it all, from the years before the war right up to the present day. They knew many of the now middle-aged characters when they were young, saw them grow and develop — they probably know plenty of Albert Square's secrets too!

The true matriarch of EastEnders is Lou Beale. Now over seventy, Lou has spent all her life in the Walford area. She has seen all the shifting fortunes of Albert Square and its inhabitants. She could write a book about the place.

Lou's pride and joy is her large family, and no matter what scrapes they get into she will defend them with her life. She is the tenant of No.45 Albert Square and living with her is her daughter Pauline and her family.

Lou's closest friends outside the family are Ethel Skinner, who she sometimes thinks is a bit potty, and Dot Cotton, who can be a bit of a trial at times.

Lou Beale is portrayed by Anna Wing. Born in Hackney in 1914, the daughter of a fruit and veg merchant, Anna learnt her craft in repertory theatres all over the country, and has since made many appearances on the stage. She has also been seen in several feature films and numerous TV series including *Comrade Dad* with George Cole, *Smiley's People* with Sir Alec Guinness and *Sorry* with Ronnie Corbett. "But my favourite role of all is that of Lou Beale," she says. "There is such a depth of character to her, and deep down she is so strong, the real backbone of the family."

Ethel Skinner was born in Camden Town in 1920. As a young woman she worked as a maid to a well-to-do family in Hackney. Her own family home was destroyed during a World War II bombing raid, and her mother and father were both killed in the tragedy.

For a while young Ethel lived with relations in Hackney, but then she married her sweetheart, William, who worked down at the docks. They moved into Albert Square in 1947.

Soon after William passed away in the early '70s, Ethel moved into the flat above Dr. Legg's surgery. She lives there rent free, in exchange for cleaning the surgery every day. Sharing Ethel's life is her beloved dog, Willy the pug.

Although she has a whole host of memories, our Ethel doesn't dwell in the past too much. In fact she keeps a constant eye on the future, for she has the gift of prophesy. Cross her palm with silver and she will tell your fortune either by palmistry or by reading the tea leaves. Sometimes she surprises herself — particularly when her predictions come true!

Ethel Skinner is portrayed by Gretchen Franklin, a true East Ender born within the sound of Bow Bells. Gretchen's parents were theatrical performers, so it was natural that she too should join the profession. In her long and successful career she has appeared in almost every branch of show-business, from vaudeville and the circus, through theatre, TV and films, to grand opera. Of Ethel, Gretchen says: "I adore her — she has a heart of gold."

Harold Legg was born in the East End in 1922, the son of a Jewish doctor. The family later moved to Finchley and the bright young Harold went to grammar school.
During the war he attended Bart's Hospital Medical School. Here the young students got plenty of practical experience by tending to the victims of Hitler's bombing raids on London, and to casualties of the fighting abroad who had been shipped back to Blighty. His own young wife was killed in the Blitz and he has remained a widower ever since.
Dr. Legg owns No. 1 Albert Square, the basement of which contains his surgery. He lets the remainder of the house to Lofty and Ethel, while he himself lives in a small flat in nearby Islington.
Over the years Dr. Legg has refused all invitations to join a group practise. Consequently his work-load is even larger than a normal NHS GP, and he finds it very difficult to keep things organised around the surgery.
But everyone in Albert Square respects the good doctor. In return he loves them and wouldn't work anywhere else in the world.

Dr. Legg is portrayed by Leonard Fenton, a native of London's East End. As a young man Leonard trained to be a civil engineer, a career which he followed throughout the war years and beyond. He then decided to become an actor and enrolled at the Webber Douglas drama school. Since then he has had a long career in theatre, TV and radio. One of his most recent TV successes was the part of Erich Gottlieb in *Shine On Harvey Moon.* Leonard lives with his wife and four children in north London. His hobby is painting in watercolours.

EastEnders Crossword

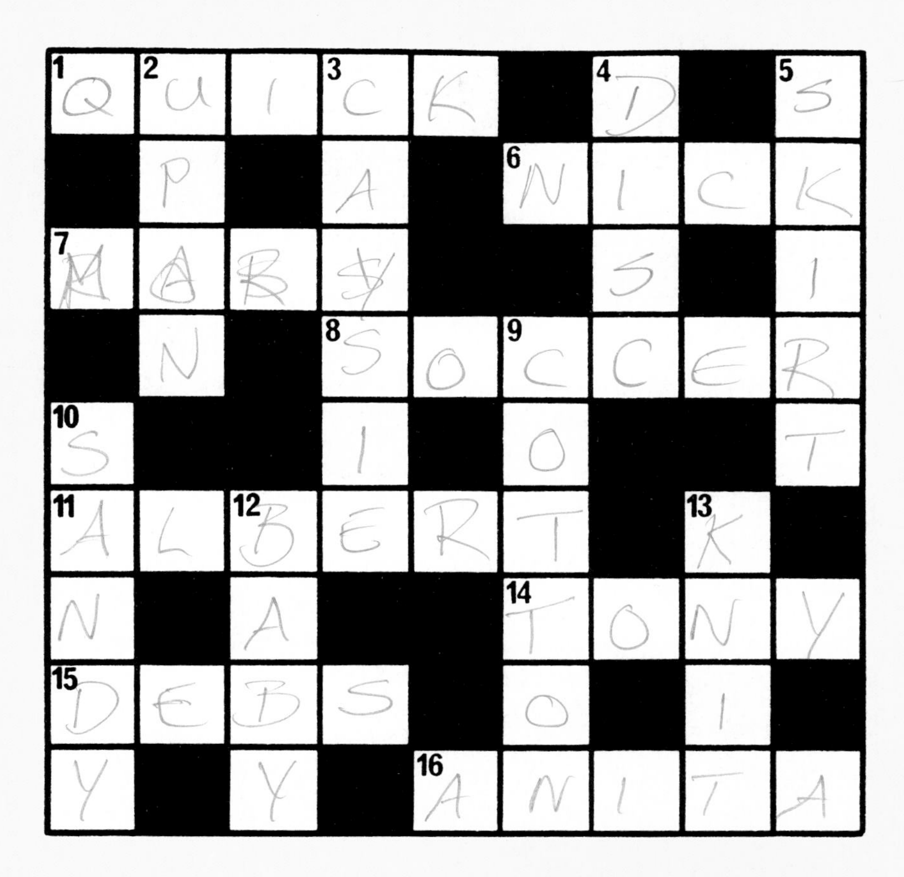

Across:

1. This detective is speedy.
6. Dot's little lad.
7. Not Linda, but ____.
8. Walford Town's game.
11. Victoria's and Lou's husband.
14. Hannah's handyman.
15. Society girls like Miss Wilkins.
16. Den is to Leslie as Angie is to ____.

Answers on page 61

Down:

2. Dot's put this by her son.
3. Smallest Carpenter in the square.
4. Arthur could slip this in the allotment if he isn't careful.
5. Walk around the edge of Albert Square.
9. Needle and Dot, perhaps.
10. Miss Ratcliffe like the beach.
12. Vicki is a cute one alright.
13. Lou's got a good reason to do this with Martin around.

Hannah

When she married Tony, the strong-willed HANNAH CARPENTER somehow expected more of him. To her way of thinking they should, by now, be living in a better part of London — or even somewhere out in the country. When her romance with Neville came to an end over his treatment of Cassie, Hannah was forced to return to Albert Square. But always at the back of her mind are thoughts of how long she'll be staying. Hannah is portrayed by Sally Sagoe.

TONY CARPENTER — played by Oscar James — arrived in England from the Caribbean when he was ten years old. He's a jobbing builder and the Albert Square handyman. Despite all the ups and downs of family life, our 'Tone' still manages to keep an optimistic outlook on things.

The EastEnders Theme

Simon May

For millions of viewers the distinctive refrain of the EastEnders theme tune signals another half hour of delightful drama. As it is played, people everywhere will stop whatever they are doing and settle down in front of the TV set.

The tune was written by Simon May and Leslie Osborne, two very experienced TV composers. Leslie had previously co-written the themes for Buccaneers and Blood Money, while Simon was responsible for the Everyman theme. Simon had also had three chart entries with songs featured in Crossroads. His most recent hit was the theme for the drama series Howards' Way.

Before working together on EastEnders, Simon and Leslie had collaborated on the Cold Warrior and Skorpion series for the BBC.

The composers' main task on EastEnders was to reflect the vitality and resilience of cockney life. "And it had to be a catchy tune," explained Simon. "One that could be heard many times without the audience tiring of it and without the music dating in any way."

If you listen closely to the EastEnders theme music, you will detect a sitar and some Caribbean drums behind the main theme.

"This was to catch a contemporary mood, and to reflect some of the ethnic influences of the multi-racial community that forms the real East End," said Simon.

The splendid result must be one of the most 'whistled' tunes of all time.

Answers

1 Q	2 U	I	3 C	K		4 D		5 S
	P		A		6 N	I	C	K
7 R	O	S	S			S		I
	N		8 S	O	9 C	C	E	R
10 S			I		O			T
11 A	L	12 B	E	R	T		13 K	
N		A			14 T	O	N	Y
15 D	E	B	S		O		I	
Y		Y		16 A	N	I	T	A

Quiz Answers

1. The little bridesmaid, age 3, is Letitia Dean now Sharon Watts.
2. The modern 'Robin Hood' is Adam Woodyatt or Ian Beale of the Tower Block, Albert Square.
3. With her brother at home in South London is Delanie Forbes, the youngest speaking member of the cast, who plays Cassie Carpenter.

1	D	11	D	21	C	31	A
2	A	12	B	22	C	32	A
3	B	13	D	23	A	33	C
4	A	14	D	24	B	34	D
5	A	15	A	25	C	35	C
6	D	16	B	26	A	36	C
7	C	17	D	27	A	37	A
8	A	18	B	28	B	38	A
9	B	19	D	29	B	39	B
10	D	20	D	30	C	40	D

How did you score?

35-40	You must live in Albert Square – Excellent.
25-34	A true EastEnders Fan-keep watching. Very good.
15-24	You keep in touch but may be missing something. Average.
Below 15	Where have you been recently? Remember Tuesdays, Thursdays and Omnibus Sundays.